Light in the Darkness
A Hanukkah Devotional for Jesus Followers

Ron Shifley

DEDICATION

This book is dedicated to our persecuted Christian brothers and sisters living in Iraq, Syria, Egypt and Libya, who like Judah Maccabeus and his fellow Jewish brethren before them, are forced to hold on to their faith in the face of intense persecution, terrorism, and martyrdom. May their faith in Jesus Christ shine like a "light in the darkness" amid a world of violence and hatred and may God use that light to help bring about a miracle of hope and deliverance for this day and age.

CONTENTS

ACKNOWLEDGMENTS

I'd like to thank Dr. Clark M. Williamson, professor of theology at Christian Theological Seminary, Indianapolis for his classes in "Post-Holocaust Theology" and "Dialogue Between Christians and Jews" for sparking my interest in the connections between Judaism and Christianity which ultimately led to my rediscovery of the biblical feasts of Israel and how they were missing in the liturgical life of the Church.

REDISCOVERING THE BIBLICAL HOLIDAY OF HANUKKAH

"It was now winter, and Jesus was in Jerusalem at the time of Hanukkah. He was at the Temple, walking through the section known as Solomon's Colonnade."
(John 10:22-23, NLT)

Don't you just hate it when you forget things? You know, like your car keys, your cell phone, or your spouse's birthday. When you realize that you forgot something, you stop. Retrace your footsteps, and hunt down the item that you left behind.

Hanukkah is an example of one of those things that has been forgotten. Hanukkah? You mean that Jewish holiday that takes place around Christmas? How could I forget it? I'm a Jesus follower. We've never celebrated Hanukkah! That's true. Most Christians have never celebrated Hanukkah, thinking that it was a Jewish holiday and taboo for Christians. The truth is, Hanukkah is a biblical holiday that's been forgotten by the Church for centuries, and it's about time that followers of Jesus not only remember it, but reclaim it and celebrate it as part of our own living faith heritage.

Hanukkah originated in 165 B.C., the period between the times that the Old Testament and New Testament were written. It celebrates the victory of Judah Maccabeus and a group of Jewish freedom fighters who beat the occupying Greek army, freed Jerusalem, and cleansed and rededicated the Temple for worship of the Lord our God.

Barney Kasdan, author of *God's Appointed Times*, recounts that "Of particular importance to them was the broken menorah, symbolizing the light of God. They restored it and attempted to light it, but there was a problem. Jewish tradition recounts that as they searched for some specially prepared oil, they found only enough to burn for one

1

day. The priests knew it would take at least eight days for new oil to be produced. What to do? They decided it was better to light the menorah anyway; at least the light of God would shine forth immediately. To their amazement, the oil burned not only for one day, but for eight days until additional oil was available."

Every year afterwards, the Jewish people celebrated the rededication of the Temple with the eight day festival of Hanukkah. Jesus, being a devout Jew, made at least one trip during his ministry to the Temple for the Hanukkah celebration (John 10:22-23). Acts 2:46 records that the Early Church continued to worship regularly at the Temple in Jerusalem, so one can assume that they would also have celebrated the annual Hanukkah (Feast of Dedication) festival for a number of years before Christianity and Judaism gradually parted ways after the destruction of the Temple in A.D. 70 when the Temple menorah was carted off to Rome as a spoil of war.

The origins of Hanukkah are recorded in the Apocryphal book of *1 Maccabees* and are summarized by the Roman historian, Flavius Josephus, in his book, *Jewish Antiquities.*

So how did we forget Hanukkah? Well, when Jews in the Holy Land revolted against Rome in A.D. 70, things ended badly. Jerusalem was burned. The Temple was destroyed, and members of the Church in Jerusalem found themselves homeless and scattered around the Roman Empire. Christianity, then a Messianic Jewish sect, tried to avoid persecution from the Roman authorities and began downplaying all things Jewish to make the Christian faith more acceptable to Roman society.

So, Hanukkah, and other biblical holidays like Passover, Purim, Feast of Tabernacles, etc. along with most of Christianity's Jewish roots gradually got tossed aside. As the Church became increasingly Gentile (non-Jewish) in membership, the biblical holidays were nearly forgotten altogether. Over time, people began to think of Hanukkah as being a Jewish holiday and not a part of Christian history, faith and practice. Jews, meanwhile, continued to celebrate this holiday as part of their religious heritage.

The funny thing is, since Hanukkah originated after the Old Testament was written, Jews don't have scriptural reference for it. Barney Kasdan notes "The people who normally celebrate this holy day, the Jewish people, have scant biblical reference for it; yet the people who do not normally celebrate Hanukkah have the most explicit reference to it, in the New Testament!"

The purpose of this book is to give the Church a resource to help reclaim and celebrate Hanukkah as a biblical holiday once again. Jesus celebrated Hanukkah. You can too! We've forgotten part of our biblical heritage for too many years. Now is the time to bring it back.

Included in this book are eight devotionals that you and your family can use together each night of Hanukkah (like all biblical holidays, Hanukkah is celebrated beginning after sunset) when you light the menorah. Make it a special time of family worship together. Read the Scripture provided. Light the appropriate number of candles on the menorah for the evening. Then read the devotional and prayer. Finally spend a few minutes either listening to or singing praise songs appropriate for the Hanukkah celebration. (A suggested YouTube music video for each night's devotion is linked via a printed QR code which can be scanned by a QR code reader app on your smart phone, iPad or other mobile device for a multi-media experience.) Afterwards, spend quality time together having fun playing the dreidel game and eating fried doughnuts. I've included instructions on how to light the Hanukkah menorah, a list of songs (both Jewish and Christian) that would be appropriate for the season, along with directions on how to play the traditional dreidel game that has become such a popular part of the holiday through the years.

Note: this book offers ways to celebrate Hanukkah from a Christian perspective. It incorporates both Jewish and Christian elements into the celebration, not to rob Jews of their holiday, but as a way for Christians to reclaim part of our biblical heritage that has been forgotten for way too long. Hanukkah belongs to both of us, Jew and Christian alike. May you be blessed in celebrating a part of your faith tradition that has been found!

MY LIGHT AND SALVATION

"The LORD is my light and salvation—whom shall I fear? The LORD is the stronghold of my life—of whom shall I be afraid? When the wicked advance against me to devour me, it is my enemies and foes who will stumble and fall. Though an army besiege me, my heart will not fear; though war break out against me, even then I will be confident.

One thing I ask from the LORD, this only do I seek; that I may dwell in the house of the LORD all the days of my life, to gaze upon the beauty of the LORD and seek him in his temple. For in the day of trouble he will keep me safe in his dwelling; he will hide me in the shelter of his sacred tent and set me high upon the rock. Then my head will be exalted above the enemies who surround me; at his sacred tent will I sacrifice with shouts of joy; I will sing and make music to the Lord." (Psalm 27:1-6)

At the core of Hanukkah is this simple truth: God is our light and salvation. When we trust in God, David writes in Psalm 27, there is nothing to fear. Even when we find ourselves up against impossible odds, we can be assured that our God will be with us and see us through.

Judah Maccabeus understood this when he led a band of Jewish freedom fighters against the Greek armies of King Antichous who not only had taken control of Judea and Jerusalem, but who was enacting laws that abolished expressing faith in the LORD our God. He saw how the Greeks tried to strip his people, his culture of their God given faith and identity. The last straw came when the Greeks dared to place and idol of the Greek god Zeus in the Temple of the LORD. That's when it happened, Judah

"Eight Nights"

StandFour

led the revolt. He would not let God be deleted from his world! Judah reminded the Jewish people of the God who stood at their side in this conflict. "Do not fear their numbers or be afraid when they charge. Remember how our fathers were saved at the Red Sea, when Pharaoh with his forces pursued them…. [For in our victory] all the Gentiles will know that there is one who redeems and saves Israel" (1 Maccabees 4:8-11). Judah believed in God's light and salvation. We light the first candle of Hanukkah this evening proclaiming that same faith.

Dear God, relight the flame of faith in my life, so that I might trust in Your strength and salvation when I find myself up against impossible odds. I need You in my life. I need a Redeemer and Savior in my life today. Help me trust in You like the Maccabees. In your Holy Name I pray. Amen.

CLEANING OUT YOUR TEMPLE

"Then said Judah and his brothers, 'Behold our enemies are crushed; let us go up to cleanse the sanctuary and dedicate it." (1 Maccabees 4:36)

"Do you not know that your bodies are temples of the Holy Spirit, who is in you, whom you have received from God? You are not your own; you were bought at a price. Therefore honor God with your bodies." (1 Corinthians 6:19-20)

Hanukkah is about cleaning. After Judah Maccabeus and his band of Jewish freedom fighters won their freedom from the Greek occupation of Judea, their first priority was to go to Jerusalem and rededicate the Temple of the LORD so that it might become a sacred space to worship God once more. The only problem was it needed cleaned first. The Temple of the LORD had been defiled by the Greeks and left in shambles.

The book of 1 Maccabees records that, "they saw the sanctuary desolate, the altar profaned, and the gates burned. In the courts they saw bushes sprung up as in a thicket... They saw also the chambers of the priests in ruins. Then they rent their clothes, and mourned with great lamentation, and sprinkled themselves with ashes. They fell face down in the ground. And when the signal was given with the trumpets, they cried out to Heaven." (1 Maccabees 4:38-40).

Why did the state of the Temple upset the Maccabees so much that they mourned as if a family member had died? They grieved because they knew that there was no way they could worship God with such filth and clutter. God deserved better. His House shouldn't be treated that way. His Temple is meant to be a holy place not

"Give Us Clean Hands"

Chris Tomlin

a garbage dump. To make it fit for God's light to shine again, it had to be cleansed of the filth, clutter and idols that had made their home there.

The Apostle Paul reminds us in 1 Corinthians that as followers of Jesus, we are to be living "temples" in which God's Spirit might dwell and shine. The problem is, too often, we let our "temples" get cluttered with so many things that we often crowd God out of our lives. How can God's light shine through us when we don't leave room for God to live in us? Hanukkah reminds us that we too need to clean out the garbage from our "temples" if we want Jesus to live in our hearts. What clutter and idols do you need to toss out to make God #1 in your life today? What garbage will be the hardest to remove?

Lord Jesus, I'm sorry for the way I let my "temple" get over run with so much clutter. As I light the candles tonight, help me cleanse my life of the filth and the grime so that Your light might shine through me again. Amen.

Third Night of Hanukkah

TURNING ON THE LIGHT

"Then they...lit the lamps on the lamp stand, and these gave light in the temple." (1 Maccabees 4:50)

"You, LORD, are my lamp; the LORD turns my darkness into light." (2 Samuel 22:29)

Don't you just hate it when the power goes out at night. Suddenly, rooms that are so familiar and cozy become foreign to us as we fumble through the darkness in places that we would walk confidently when the lights are on. Those stormy nights when the lights go out seem as if they last forever. And then, just when we wonder how long we must suffer in the darkness, the power is restored, the lights come back on, and we can go back to living out our normal routines. What a difference it is to have the lights turned back on!

The Jewish people living in Greek occupied Jerusalem must have felt like they were living through a power outage. King Antichous intended to extinguish the light and faith of the conquered Jewish people when he passed laws forbidding them from worshipping the LORD our God. Yet, even in total darkness God's Word remained "a lamp to my feet and a light for my path" (Psalm 119:105). God's people remained faithful to Scripture. It helped keep their hope and faith alive until God raised up heroes who would stand up for the LORD and fight for His name.

"Kindle a Candle of Light"

Dan Crow

What a day it must have been when Judah Maccabeus and the people gathered at the Temple, following their triumph over the Greeks and the time they spent cleaning and repairing the House of the LORD. When the priests relit the Temple menorah, the light of faith turned back on. The people realized, that just as God had not given up on Moses, David and Elijah, He was with them also, and no one could extinguish the light of the LORD our God from the earth. Darkness ended. The Light prevailed. God is light an in Him there will be no darkness that can have the final victory.

Tonight as you light the candles on the menorah, remember this simple truth of Hanukkah: Our faith cannot be extinguished even in the darkest of nights, because the Light of the World will always shine through the darkness.

Lord God, I thank you for the faith of those who relit the candles in the Temple so many years ago. It took courage to stand up for the truth and the light of Your Word. May these glowing flames remind me tonight, that in You there is light and victory. Strengthen me with Your living Word during the dark times, when faith gets extinguished., so that I can live in the light. Amen.

A LIGHT THAT WILL NOT GO OUT!

"So they celebrated the dedication of the altar for eight days…"
(1 Maccabees 4:56)

"The light shines in the darkness, and the darkness has not overcome it."
(John 1:5)

Everyday holds the possibility of a miracle. This isn't just some glib saying for positive thinkers. This is gospel truth. God can and does work miracles in our lives. Yet not every miracle is a made for Hollywood moment like when God helped Moses part the Red Sea during the Exodus. Some miracles may seem insignificant and get overlooked. Yet, when the Lord's fingerprints are seen in those moments, we ought to pause and stand in awe of God's holiness.

Hanukkah celebrates one of those minor everyday miracles. The big miracle was the way God helped to free His people from religious persecution. Then, came the small miracle. The one that seems almost too insignificant to mention, and yet remains central to celebrating the eight nights of Hanukkah is this: the lights in the Temple did not go out!

Legend has it that when the priests relit the candles of the menorah at the rededication of the Temple in 165 B.C., that there was only enough purified oil, prescribed by God in Exodus 27:20, to keep the menorah lit for one day. (It would take eight days to produce an adequate supply to keep the flame going indefinitely) Yet, the priests yearned so much for the Light of God to be re-kindled in the Temple and in people's lives, they relit it anyway.

"Open the Eyes of
My Heart"

Paul Baloche

Then it happened. God's fingerprints were made visible in the simple and the ordinary. The menorah's flame didn't die out at the end of the first day, or the second, or the third or the fourth. In fact, it remained lit for eight days until new oil could be produced. This allowed the people to celebrate God's victory, their salvation, and the Temple's rededication for eight days.

It was a simple miracle. Yet it's truth remains vital for us today as John writes in his gospel, "The light shines in the darkness, and the darkness has not overcome it." Today we don't just celebrate candles in the Temple, but the Light of the World in Jesus Christ our Lord. Like the candles of Hanukkah, the Light of Christ cannot be extinguished. The cross and empty grave prove that. His light continues to burn brightly in the lives of his followers like you and me.

Lord Jesus, as I light the candles this evening, open my eyes to see Your miracles in the everyday and the ordinary. May these simple flames remind me that Your light will shine forever and not go out. **Amen**

Fifth Night of Hanukkah

LOOKING FOR A HERO

"It was now winter, and Jesus was in Jerusalem at the time of Hanukkah. He was at the Temple, walking through the section known as Solomon's Colonnade. The Jewish leaders surrounded him and asked, 'How long are you going to keep us in suspense? If you are the Messiah, tell us plainly.'"
(John 10:22-24, NLT)

"When Jesus spoke again to the people, he said, 'I am the light of the world. Whoever follows me will never walk in darkness, but will have the light of life.'"
(John 8:12)

Jesus was at the Temple for the Festival of Hanukkah when it happened. The religious leaders surrounded him and asked, "How long are you going to keep us in suspense? If you are the Messiah, tell us plainly." They were looking for a hero. Only 195 years after the Maccabees had liberated Jerusalem from the Greeks, the country was now under Roman occupation. Hanukkah, the Festival of Dedication, was a time when people looked for a Messiah, a Savior, to come and set them free. Could Jesus be the one? Could he really?

Jesus stood in the same Temple that Judah Maccabeus had cleansed and rededicated back to the worship of the LORD our God. This was where the miracle had occurred so many years ago. People were looking for a new miracle, a new hero, a fresh anointing from God for today. So are we. Our world clamors for a hero, for light to pierce through the darkness and bring rescue in these troubled times. The exciting news of Hanukkah is that our hero, our deliverance has already come!

Jesus proclaimed to the crowds, "I am the light of the world." He is the miracle

"Mighty to Save"

Jeremy Camp

sent from God to free the captives from a darkness greater than Roman occupation: the darkness of sin and death. Jesus came to bring light and life to all who would believe on his name. He is the hero for which we seek. Messianic Jews note that every Hanukkah menorah has a ninth candle, raised above the rest, that lights the rest of the candles each night. That candle is called the Servant Candle. That candle represents Jesus the Messiah, who came like a servant (Philippians 2:7), and gives us the light of God's salvation. Celebrate Him, and His saving grace, when you light the candles this evening.

Lord, Jesus, I just want to thank You during this Hanukkah season, for coming as the Light of the World. Thank You for giving all of us the "light of life." Help me, Lord, to share Your light with those looking for heroes to dispel the darkness of our present age. In Your name I pray. Amen.

Sixth Night of Hanukkah

ARE YOU WALKING IN THE LIGHT?

"...God is light; in him there is no darkness at all. If we claim to have fellowship with him yet walk in the darkness, we lie and do not live out the truth. But if we walk in the light, as he is in the light, we have fellowship with one another, and the blood of Jesus, his Son, purifies us from all sin."
(1 John 1:5-7)

Folks in Jerusalem had a tough choice to make after King Antichous made laws that forbade God's people from worshipping Him and living out their faith in their everyday lives. Should they give in to the king's demands, give up their faith and fit in? Or should they stand up for the LORD no matter what? This was a tough choice. Breaking the law could lead to imprisonment or death. Giving up one's faith meant a life lived in peace and quiet.

We face those same choices today when media and pop culture ridicule people for having faith in God. Some find it easier to fit in. They may go to church on Sunday, but hide their Jesus follower identity the rest of the week so they don't get harassed by peers at work or in school. The only problem with that is when we "walk in the darkness, we lie and do not live out the truth" (1 John 1:6). Covering up our faith to fit in means, in essence, that we extinguish the Light of Christ from our everyday lives.

So how did God's people handle this choice in the time of the Maccabees? Legend has it that some of God's people chose to gather and study the Scriptures even though it was illegal. They'd gather in groups to study the Torah (the first five books of the Old Testament), but when Greek soldiers passed by, they'd

"Burn"

The Maccabeats

hide their Torah scrolls and spin dreidels, so that it looked like they were gambling. This was an act of defiance even if it was done in secret. Others, like Judah Maccabeus and his father, the old priest Mattathias, lived their faith "in the light" and refused to give in to peer pressure at all. They chose to walk in the light no matter the cost. Hanukkah celebrates the defiant faith of God's people who choose to walk in the light of the LORD.

How do you handle this tough choice of faith? Do you choose to walk in the light or to hide your faith identity when peer pressure gets too strong? Think about those choices during these days of Hanukkah.

Lord Jesus, as I light these candles tonight, I realize that I am faced with a choice. It's a tough choice. I thank God for the example of the Maccabees who chose to "walk in the light" even when it was unpopular. Lord, I want to be a bolder disciple in my world today. Light a flame of boldness in my life so that Your light shines forth everyday and everywhere. Amen.

Seventh Night of Hanukkah

A LIGHT GLOWING INSIDE OF ME

"No one has ever seen God; but if we love one another; God lives in us and his love is made complete in us. This is how we know that we live in him and he in us: He has given us of his Spirit. And we have seen and testify that the Father has sent his Son to be the Savior of the world." (1 John 4:12-14)

While Hanukkah is a festive holiday celebrating light, faith and hope, it is also a holiday that is celebrated with a tinge of sadness as well. The Temple in Jerusalem, that the Maccabees liberated and rededicated and in which Jesus our Lord celebrated the festival during his ministry, was destroyed by Rome in A.D. 70. With the Temple gone, some wonder, why celebrate Hanukkah at all?

We celebrate Hanukkah today for one simple reason. We have become the living "temples" of the LORD. The Apostle Paul reminds us that we, who have accepted Jesus in our hearts, have become "a temple of the Holy Spirit, who is in you..." (1 Corinthians 6:19). Just as the candles were lit in the Temple by the Maccabees, to show the world that God's light and love were alive in Jerusalem, we light these candles of Hanukkah tonight to remind us that, if God lives in us, then our lives need to become a place where the light of the LORD burns brightly.

Your life has been liberated by Jesus the Messiah and cleansed by the blood of the Lamb so that you might become a living "temple" of the LORD, where His Holy Spirit dwells. As a sanctuary of the LORD, you are called to be the holy place where God's light and love shine brightly in this dark and troubled world. Hanukkah reminds us, that just as the Temple in Jerusalem needed to be rededicated for God's light

"Better Is One Day"

Matt Redman

and glory to dwell, so too we need to daily rededicate our lives to Jesus so that the Light of the World might brightly burn within our souls.

Is the Holy Spirit glowing inside of me? Have I taken the time to kindle the light of His love in my life? Do people see the light of Christ glowing in me, and does that light cause them to worship Him? These are important questions for all of us to ask during these nights of Hanukkah.

Lord Jesus, as I light the candles of Hanukkah this evening, I do so with joy, for I want to be Your living sanctuary, where Your Spirit and glory dwells. Like the candles lit by the Maccabees so many years ago, I want to shine as a miracle, of what life can be like, when Your love lives in someone like me. So, Lord Jesus, I give You my heart and life this evening. Come live inside of me. Shine through me, and my love, so that others might be drawn to You, worship You, and give their lives to You, This is my prayer. Amen.

Eighth Night of Hanukkah

A LIGHT FOR ALL TO SEE

"You are the light of the world. A town built on a hill cannot be hidden. Neither do people light a lamp and put it under a bowl. Instead they put it on its stand, and it gives light to everyone in the house. In the same way, let your light shine before others, that they may see your good deeds and glorify your Father in heaven." (Matthew 5:14-16)

One of the Jewish traditions of Hanukkah is to place their Hanukkah menorah near the windows of their homes. That way when they light the menorah each night during Hanukkah, people passing by can be reminded of the miracle of God's light and salvation. This Hanukkah tradition is reminiscent of Jesus' words from Matthew 5:16, "...let your light shine before others, that they may see your good deeds and glorify your Father in heaven."

The light of Christ that we have received is not for us alone. To keep God's light and salvation all to ourselves is to squander God's gift. Jesus instructs us not to hide His light or keep it a secret from others. Instead, he instructs us to let his light and our faith shine so that "it gives light to everyone in the house," and to everyone who passes by at school, at work, at the grocery story or the shopping mall. We are to be "the light of the world" and let God's love shine through us everywhere.

"Eight Nights"

StandFour

How brightly is your light shining this evening? Who's seen it shine this past week? Who needs to see it? How will you continue to kindle the flame of God's love in the days ahead?

So here we are, on the last night of Hanukkah. As you kindle the final candle on the menorah, pause and remember, the faith of the Maccabees so many years ago, what cleaning it takes to make our "temples" fit for God's light to shine, the joy that comes when we let God shine in our lives, that this light cannot be extinguished, and that Jesus has come not only as our Messiah, but as the Light of the World. Because of this, we have choices to make. Will we walk in the light? Will we open ourselves to become a living "temple" for the LORD and will we let our lights shine for all to see?

These eight nights of Hanukkah are an important season of reflection. Yet, these nights of Hanukkah are only the beginning. Your "temple" needs regular inspection, cleansing and rededication to allow God's light to shine in you throughout the year. May the lessons of Hanukkah enable you to begin a deeper faith walk with Christ Jesus our Lord.

Lord Jesus, I thank you for these eight nights of Hanukkah. Help me, I pray, to let your light shine in my life for all the world to see. Open my eyes to see people who need Your amazing grace and challenge me to shine, even in dark places, so that Your light might give life and hope to everyone. Amen.

HOW TO LIGHT THE HANUKKAH MENORAH

The central observance in Hanukkah is the lighting of the nine candle Hanukkah menorah at sundown. The menorah, which symbolizes the one in the Jerusalem Temple, is lit one candle at a time for eight nights to celebrate the eight nights during the Temple's rededication that God caused one day's supply of purified oil to burn for eight days straight.

Hanukkah menorahs are lit around the world at both large, public venues like churches, synagogues, or the Temple Mount in Jerusalem and in small, private family ceremonies at believer's homes.

At the center of the Hanukkah menorah is a ninth candle lifted above the others, called the "Servant Candle," that is used to light the other eight candles. Messianic Jews claim the "Servant Candle" represents Jesus the Messiah who came as a servant who gives light to all who allow themselves to shine for God (Matthew 20:28, John 1:9, John 8:12)

Video of Hanukkah menorah lighting at the Western Wall of the Temple Mount in Jerusalem

Candles are placed on the menorah from right to left according to the number of nights that one is currently at during the eight day festival. For example: on the first night of Hanukkah only one candle is lit in addition to the "Servant Candle." On the second night, two candles are lit, and so on, and so on. Candles are lit from left to right, using the "Servant Candle," so that the newest day's candle is lit first. Then the previous nights' candles are lit afterward.

Did You Know? The Temple menorah, upon which the Hanukkah menorah is based, was originally designed by God for use in the Tabernacle. The lamp stand is described in Exodus 25:31-39. Exodus 27:20-21 describes the divine mandate for the oil to be used: "Command the Israelites to bring you clear oil of pressed olives for the light so that the lamps may be kept burning...This is to be a lasting ordinance among the Israelites for the generations to come." The priests, during the Temple's rededication at the time of the Maccabees, sought to fulfill God's command to only use purified oil to light the Temple menorah. The shortage of such oil set the stage for the legendary miracle of oil upon which the lighting of the Hanukkah menorah for eight nights during the annual holiday is based.

HOW TO PLAY THE DREIDEL GAME

One of the fun traditions of Hanukkah is the dreidel game. A dreidel is a four-sided spinning top that families play with during the eight nights of Hanukkah. Each side is imprinted with a Hebrew letter. These letters are an acronym for the Hebrew words (Nes Gadol Haya Sham), "A great miracle happened there", referring to the legendary miracle of the oil that took place at the Temple in Jerusalem.

The dreidel game is played to commemorate the time when biblical faith was outlawed by King Antiochus Epiphanes from 168-165 B.C. and the reading and teaching of Scripture was forbidden. Yet, legend has it that faithful Jews continued to teach God's Word in small groups. When Greek soldiers would pass by, the Jews would hide their Torah scrolls and begin spinning the dreidel so that it would appear that they were gambling and not studying Scripture.

The game is played using a dreidel and chocolate coins (gelt) usually imprinted with an image of the menorah on them. (These coins are reminiscent of national coins minted by the Maccabees which celebrated their freedom from the Greeks. The ancient coins featured an image of the Temple menorah minted on one side. Thus, current Hanukkah gelt coins celebrate that heritage.)

Each player starts out with 10 or 15 coins and places one coin in the "pot." The first player spins the dreidel, and depending on which side the dreidel falls on, either wins a coin from the pot or gives up part of his or her stash. The code is as follows:

- Nun–"none"–the player gets none and the next player spins
- Gimel–"all"–the player gets all the coins in the pot. Each player then puts one coin in to replenish the pot.
- Hey–"half"–the player takes half of the pot, rounding up if there is an odd number
- Shin–"put one in"–each player puts one coin in the pot

Play continues until one player wins the entire pot of coins. After the game is over, all the coins are divided up evenly so each player has their own chocolate coins to enjoy.

A meaningful variation of the game might be to include Scripture memorization while players are participating in the game. That way everyone has a chance to experience the context of how this legendary game originated. Any of the Bible verses included in the daily devotions would be appropriate for use.

FESTIVE HANUKKAH FOODS

It is a custom to eat foods either cooked or fried in oil during the eight nights of Hanukkah as another way to remember how the one jar of purified oil, found in the Temple after it was liberated by the Maccabees, was used to relight the menorah and by a miracle of God the menorah lights kept burning for eight days until new oil could be made. Traditional Hanukkah foods include potato pancakes called "latkes" that are fried in oil and homemade doughnuts, deep fried in oil, that are either dipped in cinnamon and sugar or filled with fluff, custard or fruit filling.

SUGGESTED SONGS FOR HANUKKAH CELEBRATION

Here is a listing of Jewish and Christian praise songs that are appropriate for Hanukkah worship and celebration. All of the songs are available on YouTube for viewing with your smart phone, tablet or personal computer. Most of the songs are also available for purchase on iTunes or CD as well.

Jewish Hanukkah Songs

"Burn" by Maccabeats from the album, *One Day More*. 2014.

"Candlelight" by Maccabeats from the single *Candlelight*. 2010.

"Eight Candles" by Malvina Reynolds from the album *Chanukah at Home*. 1998.

"Eight Nights" by StandFour from the original music video single *Eight Nights*. 2012.

"Kindle a Candle of Light" by Dan Crow from the album *Chanukah at Home*. 1998.

"Rock of Ages (Maoz Tsur)" traditional from the album *Chanukah at Home*. 1998.

Christian Praise Songs

"Better Is One Day" by Matt Redman from the album *Blessed Be Your Name*. 1995.

"Give Us Clean Hands" by Charlie Hall from the album *It Is Well*. 2009.

"God of This City" by Chris Tomlin from the album *Hello Love*. 2008.

"Here I Am to Worship" by Tim Hughes from the album *Here I Am to Worship*. 2001.

"Hear Us From Heaven" by Ross Parsley from the album *I Am Free*. 2005.

"Mighty to Save" by Ben Fielding & Reuben Morgan from the album *Mighty to Save*. 2010.

"Open The Eyes of My Heart" by Paul Baloche from the album *Open the Eyes of My Heart*. 2000.

WHERE CAN I FIND HANUKKAH RESOURCES?

It doesn't take a lot to celebrate the biblical holiday of Hanukkah. The essentials are a nine-branch Hanukkah menorah, Hanukkah candles, a dreidel and chocolate coins (gelt). Hanukkah party supplies like plates, napkins, etc. are also available if you want to host a Hanukkah theme party at your home or church.

Hanukkah menorahs can be purchased in many designs, traditional and contemporary, made out of either metal, stone or glass, for use with candles or olive oil. There are even menorahs designed just for children. Hanukkah menorahs and candles can be purchased at all of the following online retailers. Christian Book Distributers does not carry dreidels or chocolate coins (gelt).

- · Bargain Judaica (www.bargainjudaica.com)
- · Hanukkah Sale (www.hanukkahsale.com)
- · Chocolate Gelt (www.chocolategelt.com)
- · eBay (www.ebay.com)
- · Christian Book Distributers (www.christianbook.com)

Looking for additional games to play during Hanukkah? Check out these games that use the classic dreidel in new ways. They are available at various online retailers.

· *Maccabees Board Game*—Lead a band of Maccabees to acquire enough oil to relight the Temple menorah.

· *Staccabees*—Build a tower with wood blocks, kind of like the game of Jenga only played with a dreidel.

ABOUT THE AUTHOR

Rev. Ron Shifley is an ordained pastor in the Evangelical Association of Reformed & Congregational Christian Churches (EA) where he serves on the National Board of Directors and its Web Ministry Team. A graduate of Christian Theological Seminary, Indianapolis, he has served local congregations in Indiana, Ohio and South Dakota. He and his wife, Deanna, have one grown daughter and two grandchildren.

Made in the USA
Columbia, SC
22 November 2022

71945467R00020